Mediterranean Security

New Issues and Challenges

Conference Proceedings

Brussels

October 15–17, 1995

T0167457

F. Stephen Larrabee

Carla Thorson

RAND

An International Conference Organized by RAND with the support of the NATO Office of Information and Press

PREFACE

On October 15–17, 1995, RAND, in conjunction with the NATO Office of Information and Press, held a conference in Brussels on Mediterranean security issues. The conference was attended by some ninety government officials, academics, and specialists representing NATO member countries, non-NATO Mediterranean countries, and international organizations. The non-NATO Mediterranean dialogue countries participating were Egypt, Israel, Mauritania, Morocco, and Tunisia. Representatives from the European Union, the North Atlantic Assembly, NATO, and the Western European Union also participated.

The conference was cosponsored by RAND and the NATO Office of Information and Press. Additional funding was provided by the National Defense Research Institute at RAND and the RAND European-American Center for Policy Analysis located in Delft, the Netherlands, which also provided administrative support for the conference.

CONTENTS

Preface   iii

Summary   vii

Acknowledgments   xi

INTRODUCTION   1

MEDITERRANEAN SECURITY: NEW ISSUES AND
    CHALLENGES   3

THE SECURITY ENVIRONMENT IN THE MEDITERRANEAN:
    WESTERN VIEWS   9

NON-NATO PERSPECTIVES   15

ECONOMIC DEVELOPMENT AND DEMOCRATIZATION   17

CRISIS PREVENTION: THE ROLE OF WESTERN
    INSTITUTIONS   21

NATO'S ROLE IN THE MEDITERRANEAN   25

LIST OF PARTICIPANTS   29

AGENDA   37

On October 15–17, 1995, RAND, in conjunction with the NATO Office of Information and Press, held a conference in Brussels on Mediterranean security issues. The conference was attended by some ninety government officials, academics, and specialists representing NATO member countries, non-NATO Mediterranean countries, and international organizations. The non-NATO Mediterranean dialogue countries participating were Egypt, Israel, Mauritania, Morocco, and Tunisia. Representatives from the European Union, the North Atlantic Assembly, NATO, and the Western European Union also took part in the conference.

This report summarizes the results of the conference. The report is not intended to be a detailed account of the sessions, but rather to highlight key issues and perspectives that emerged during the proceedings.

KEY FINDINGS

- The main challenges to security in the Mediterranean are economic and political. They arise out of the lack of economic development on the one hand, and the lack of political legitimacy of many of the governments in the region on the other. In many instances, therefore, the European Union (EU) is in a better position than NATO to contain and manage these challenges.

- Economic change is a fundamental necessity. If the countries of the region are unable to manage their economic problems, there will be serious political and social upheavals that could spill over into Europe. Thus, Europe has no choice but to help these countries foster economic growth and promote political liberalization.

- Economic underdevelopment, combined with growing demographic pressures, is creating strong pressures for migration to Europe. The dimensions of this problem have increased significantly in recent years. As a consequence, Europe needs to rethink its aid and immigration policies.

- Islamic extremism should be clearly differentiated from political Islam. The threat to stability in the Mediterranean littoral comes not from Islamic politics per se but from Islamic radicalism and extremism, which have gained strength because of the inability of many of the countries in the region to deal effectively with their mounting economic and social problems.

- It is important for NATO to avoid giving the impression that it considers Islam per se to represent a new ideological threat to NATO or the West. Such an impression will only reinforce existing suspicions in many non-NATO dialogue countries (Israel excepted) and make any political dialogue between NATO and the political elite in these countries more difficult.

- Turkey's role in the region is growing. It stands at the crossroads connecting three areas—the Balkans, the Caucasus, and the Middle East—that vitally influence Mediterranean security. Europe, therefore, should do more to strengthen Turkey's European orientation and its ties to Europe.

- While the EU-Mediterranean partnership is evidence of the EU's desire to play a more active role in the Mediterranean, the lack of a broad unified policy toward the region prevents Europe from playing a more effective role in the region.

- NATO's effort to extend stability cannot be limited to the East. It must be complemented by an effort to extend stability to the South as well. However, NATO's outreach to the South needs to be tailored to the specific political and cultural environment that exists in the Middle East and North Africa.

- NATO has an image problem among the dialogue states. Many elites—as well as publics generally—in the dialogue countries remain strongly suspicious of NATO. They fear that NATO's interest in the Mediterranean is prompted by a search for a "new enemy" now that the Soviet threat has disappeared. Hence, cooperation with the non-NATO dialogue countries needs to address this problem.

- In its initial stage, NATO's Mediterranean Initiative should concentrate on educating elites in the dialogue countries about NATO's purposes and goals and changing their image of NATO. If these efforts prove successful, they could be followed by attempts to develop defense cooperation in concrete areas at a later date.

- NATO needs a better understanding of the views and perceptions of the non-NATO dialogue countries. What do they really want from NATO? How do they wish to see their relationship with NATO develop? These issues need more systematic research and analysis in order for NATO to develop a more informed policy.

- NATO's command structure, including the role of AFSOUTH, needs to be streamlined and reorganized. The command structure is largely a function of the Cold War and still remains too heavily oriented toward the Central Front. However, the main security challenges facing the Alliance today are not on the Central Front but on Europe's periphery and beyond Europe's borders. NATO's command structure therefore needs to be reorganized in order to enhance NATO's capacity to deal more effectively with these challenges.

- The United States continues to play an important strategic role in the Mediterranean. As the EU develops a more comprehensive policy toward the Mediterranean, new ways need to be found to engage the United States without inhibiting or compromising Europe's own interests.

ACKNOWLEDGMENTS

The authors would like to thank Barbara Kliszewski and Carole Simms of the RAND Santa Monica staff; Loes Romeijn and Mathilde van't Hoog of the RAND European-American Center for Policy Analysis in Delft, the Netherlands; and Nicola de Santis of the NATO Office of Information and Press for their valuable assistance in helping arrange the conference. The authors would also like to thank RAND colleagues Jerrold Green and Ian Lesser for their helpful comments in the preparation of the conference report.

INTRODUCTION

On October 15–17, 1995, RAND, in conjunction with the NATO Office of Information and Press, held a conference on Mediterranean security issues. The conference was attended by some ninety government officials, academics, and specialists representing NATO member countries, non-NATO Mediterranean countries, and international organizations. The non-NATO Mediterranean dialogue countries participating were Egypt, Israel, Mauritania, Morocco, and Tunisia. Representatives from the European Union, the North Atlantic Assembly, NATO, and the Western European Union also participated in the conference.

The two days of discussions were organized into four sessions. The first session examined Western views of Mediterranean security. Session two focused on non-NATO perspectives on Mediterranean security and considered the implications of economic, political, and social change for security in the region. The third session addressed issues of crisis prevention and what types of political and institutional arrangements could most effectively manage security problems in the region. The final session examined the influence of developments in neighboring regions, particularly the Balkans and the Middle East, on the Mediterranean, and sought to develop guidelines for future policy.

This summary of the conference proceedings is organized around the major themes that emerged during the two days of discussions in Brussels. It is not intended to be a detailed account of the sessions, but rather to highlight key issues and perspectives raised during the conference. It also includes the keynote address by Ambassador Sergio Balanzino, Deputy Secretary General of NATO.

MEDITERRANEAN SECURITY:
NEW ISSUES AND CHALLENGES

Keynote Address
Ambassador Sergio Balanzino
Deputy Secretary General of NATO

I am very pleased to be here this morning to make the keynote remarks, on behalf of the secretary general, at the opening of this seminar sponsored jointly by RAND and NATO. I believe the seminar is a very useful and timely one: We need to encourage greater Mediterranean dialogue between the countries on both of its shores. And we need to gather experts and interested parties together to address dispassionately the important issues of Mediterranean security in the post–Cold War era.

NATO's support for this event is an indication of a growing realization that the security of Europe cannot be divorced from countries of the southern Mediterranean. In a sense, NATO has always had a close interest in the region. There are six Mediterranean member countries of the Alliance, and they enjoy a security guarantee under the Washington Treaty. As we all know, under Article V, the Allies have an obligation to defend each other against armed attack and to restore and maintain their security.

For the past 40 years, this obligation was seen largely in the light of a massive Soviet threat. Today, we do not consider ourselves to be under threat of attack either from the East or from other directions. The lifting of the Iron Curtain has changed fundamentally the nature of European and even world politics. And NATO is changing with it. We have moved from confrontation to cooperation and partnership with the countries of Central and Eastern Europe, including with Russia and the other countries on the territory of the former Soviet Union.

The most visible and substantial achievements are certainly those in Central and Eastern Europe. Despite the difficulties of the transition process to democracy and market economy of the former communist states, a general mood of optimism prevails there, in part because of the role NATO is playing in projecting security to the East.

The end of East-West confrontation has also had its positive impact in the Mediterranean, as the tensions resulting from that confrontation, which also affected that area, have eased and almost disappeared. But both the Gulf War and the war in the former Yugoslavia have reminded us that the issue of Mediterranean security extends well beyond the end of the Cold War. It is thus quite appropriate that the Mediterranean has become a greater focus of NATO attention.

Since our landmark Brussels Summit in January of last year we have sought to develop a more specific approach towards Mediterranean security. In December 1994, our foreign ministers decided to establish contacts, on a case-by-case basis, between the Alliance and the Mediterranean nonmember countries. In February of this year, the Council decided to invite Egypt, Israel, Mauritania, Morocco, and Tunisia to discuss possible participation in this dialogue.

In the initial discussion we briefed the representatives of these five countries on NATO's new agenda and sought their views on Mediterranean security issues. We have since then held follow-up meetings and are currently discussing the way ahead. We hope that further discussion will lead to the establishment of a permanent dialogue with them and, let me emphasize, we hope in time to extend the initiative to other Mediterranean countries.

This manifestation of NATO's increasing interest in stability in and around the Mediterranean should not, however, be misconstrued. Let me state clearly that NATO does not see Islam as a threat, and does not need to find a new role or conjure up new threats to keep itself busy. The Mediterranean is not a horizontal dividing line, separating the European North from an "arc of crisis" in the African South. The Mediterranean Sea links three continents. Quite naturally, therefore, it is a region of tremendous cultural and religious diversity. This pluralism is an asset: Complexity is not synonymous with "threat" or "disorder."

The first point, therefore, I would like to make is that a great value of any debate about Mediterranean security is that it should dispel the clouds of misunderstanding, deliberate myth-making, and sheer ignorance in which much discussion of this subject has become shrouded. This is not easy. The human mind likes to simplify things, and for some it has become tempting to project the East-West pattern of the Cold War to other regions. So, the clash of ideologies of the Cold War has now reemerged in new academic clothes as a "clash of civilizations."

While these views may still be fashionable in some quarters, reality— as so often—is already proving them wrong. The Atlantic Alliance itself is an example of how diversity can mean strength and not antagonism. In NATO we are made up of sixteen countries of diverse cultures and different religious traditions, including one Moslem country, which have worked together for our common mutual benefit for more than four decades. The real world is much more sophisticated, much less fractured, and infinitely more capable of real cooperation than some wish to admit.

That brings me to the second value of a conference such as this one. That is, it can identify and underline how much we have in common. Indeed, how much our interests coincide rather than clash.

We certainly believe that there is a great benefit in an intensified and expanding Mediterranean dialogue. You will receive tomorrow a detailed briefing on NATO's Mediterranean initiative. Let me just say at this point that we undertook to develop our relationship out of a positive belief in the mutual value of friendship across the Mediterranean.

Some may view skeptically the importance of "soft" diplomacy. But I think it is wrong to underestimate the power of such dialogue and its potential to stimulate and develop constructive and deepening cooperation. In fact, all the major developments associated with the end of the Cold War, from German unity to NATO's deepening relationship with Russia, began with dialogue. In Europe, the examples can be multiplied. To understand how powerful dialogue can be as an instrument of change, you only have to look at the development of the CSCE, which began tentatively as a forum for discussion across a geographically and ideologically divided Europe. Now it is a full-fledged organization, building its own capacity for conflict prevention.

The history of NATO's outreach to its East since 1990 is another vivid example of how dialogue can expand and lead to something much deeper. Since 1994, we have seen how Partnership for Peace has fed on its own success so that it now far exceeds all initial expectations.

Of course, our Mediterranean initiative occurs in the context of many other challenges facing the Alliance—enlargement, our relationship with Russia, and NATO-WEU relations. Yet, there is much we can contribute to more friendly relations in the Mediterranean. That is why we have initiated a tailor-made dialogue which, drawing on successful concepts which have been applied elsewhere, begins with initial contacts and has the potential to grow. Our foremost initial aim is to make NATO as transparent and understandable as possible to our counterparts in the Mediterranean region. We have started, but our initiative still has some way to go before we reach the degree of understanding we would like.

I would note that NATO's efforts are intended to complement other initiatives, including those by the EU and WEU. In this regard, the Alliance has unique capacity and expertise, particularly in underlining the transatlantic dimension of security cooperation. We have a proven track record in bringing together countries of such different security backgrounds to serve the common interest of peace and stability. It would thus be paradoxical indeed if we did not try to develop our relations with countries in the Mediterranean who share a common interest with us in promoting a peaceful and friendly security environment.

That brings me to the third positive value of this conference. It will allow us to put the problems and challenges of the Mediterranean in their proper context.

Analysts point to the many conflicts, real and potential, that originate in or have an impact on the area. Yes, it is true that numerous conflicts reverberate throughout the area and beyond. The Bosnian conflict, for example, has had a powerful impact on attitudes among the Islamic states. We still struggle with the aftershocks of the Gulf War. And we will have to find an answer to the pressing problem of the proliferation of weapons of mass destruction and their delivery means. I would note, however, that the recent successes of the Middle East peace process remind us that to view the Mediterranean region as one huge potential crisis area is unjustified.

The steps towards a resolution of the Bosnian conflict, which NATO is seeking to help bring about, constitute further indication of a momentum in the right direction.

So, ladies and gentlemen, let me conclude. The new Mediterranean initiatives and projects such as this conference are part of a growing involvement and interest in the Mediterranean region by NATO and other arrangements supported by the EU and the WEU. Greater understanding in itself is a stimulus for a virtuous circle of increasing contact and a more far-reaching cooperation. I am sure that the next two days will prove most profitable in all these areas and I hope I have given you a clear idea of how important a subject we in the Alliance believe this to be.

The secretary general and I very much look forward to hearing your conclusions.

THE SECURITY ENVIRONMENT IN THE MEDITERRANEAN: WESTERN VIEWS

The initial session of the conference focused on the changing security environment in the Mediterranean. What do we mean when we refer to the Mediterranean? Does it, in fact, make sense to talk about "Mediterranean security?"

Most conference participants agreed that it is difficult to analyze the Mediterranean as a single unit. The area is too fragmented. A French participant suggested that there are really four different security issues in the region:

- the Maghreb,

- the Balkans,

- the Greek-Turkish dispute, and

- the Arab-Israeli conflict.

During the Cold War, Mediterranean issues were largely left outside the main competition between the superpowers. The Arab-Israeli conflict is the only area where there was deep superpower involvement.

The primary problem today, the French participant argued, is the Maghreb. Islamic fundamentalism poses a major problem because of the danger of the extension of terrorism and civil war to the European continent. Algeria is a major potential flashpoint. Conflict there could send shock waves throughout the Arab world. It poses a particular problem for France because of the large number of Algerians living in France and the possibility of increased terrorism against French nationals. In addition, if the situation in Algeria continues to deteriorate, it could create a major immigration problem, especially for France.

The Balkans, strictly speaking, are not a Mediterranean issue. But developments there, several speakers pointed out, could have—indeed, are having—strong reverberations throughout the Mediterranean. Witness the important impact that the Bosnian conflict is having on many Islamic states in North Africa and the Middle East. The Balkans are thus part of the larger Mediterranean equation. Moreover, Greece and Turkey, both Mediterranean states, have strong interests there. The turmoil in the Balkans has exacerbated bilateral Greek-Turkish differences and given them a sharper edge. This is another illustration of how Mediterranean security and Balkan security have become closely linked in the post–Cold War era.

The fragmentation of the Mediterranean and the difficulty of defining it as a distinct security problem or entity were a central theme throughout the conference. One American participant suggested that there are three different ways to think about Mediterranean security. First, there is a traditional view, which sees the Mediterranean as an extension of the European environment. It defines developments around the Mediterranean in terms of their impact on European security and transatlantic relations. One aspect of this issue is military, but this seems inadequate, he suggested, when one considers that the problems in the Mediterranean are more social and economic and generally involve South-South conflicts rather than North-South conflicts.

The second approach is to view the Mediterranean as "the place where the Persian Gulf begins." This approach emphasizes the economic and logistical dimensions of security, especially the sea lines of communication and the role of facilities in the southern region in supporting operations beyond the Mediterranean littoral. In the Gulf War, for instance, 90 percent of the material that went to the Gulf went through the Mediterranean. Also, one cannot isolate the Middle East from events taking place in Bosnia and in North Africa or vice versa. Regional events have an impact on the Muslim world as a whole as well as on the way Europeans view the Muslim world. The Middle East peace process is also influenced by Mediterranean developments.

The third approach is to think of the Mediterranean as a region in transition. Some have suggested that the Mediterranean is an "arc of crisis." However, it may be more fruitful to think of it as an "arc of change." Rapid political and social change is taking place in this region and at least two of the crisis points—Algeria and Turkey—are very much products of this transformation process. Algeria is not just a regional issue. It has very important transatlantic dimensions and broader geopolitical implications because different Alliance members have different interests. This makes Algeria an issue for the EU and, to some extent, for NATO. Similarly, Turkey's evolution will have a significant impact on security in the Mediterranean as well as on transatlantic relations more generally. The key issue is whether Turkey will serve as a bridge or barrier in strategic terms.

Turkey's role in the Mediterranean has increased since the end of the Cold War. In light of this, several participants questioned whether it was prudent to keep Turkey out of the EU. However, few countries in Europe support Turkey's entry into the EU. The official explanation is that Turkey is not ready economically to join the EU. But, as several participants emphasized, cultural and religious factors also play an important role, even though few European officials are willing to admit this publicly. The European left also has strong reservations about Turkey's human rights record. These problems notwithstanding, there was a strong consensus among participants that a stable, democratic Turkey is critical for stability in the Eastern Mediterranean and that more should be done to ensure Turkey's European orientation and to strengthen Turkey's ties to Europe.

One American participant pointed out that the Greek-Turkish dispute not only affects Mediterranean security but also has an important impact on NATO and transatlantic relations. It is important, in his words, "to get both the East and the South right." A new conflict between Greece and Turkey would have consequences not only for security in the Mediterranean but also for NATO enlargement. Many European members of NATO are worried about "importing new Greek-Turkish disputes" into the Alliance. Renewed conflict between Greece and Turkey would reinforce those concerns and could weaken support for enlargement.

At the same time, the distinction between Middle Eastern and Mediterranean security, several participants suggested, is breaking down. It is thus less and less useful to talk about these areas, and the security problems associated with them, separately. Similarly, the place of southern European concerns in transatlantic relations is changing. It is no longer possible to neatly divide roles in the region so that the United States has responsibility for military security and the Europeans look after economic security. In addition, the U.S. role is changing. In the early 1990s, the United States was reserved— at best—about multilateral approaches to Mediterranean security, such as the CSCM proposal. However, since then, several American participants argued, the U.S. attitude has evolved, and today Washington's attitude toward such initiatives is much more positive. Witness the U.S. support for the Barcelona conference.

Perceptions about Mediterranean security are changing within Europe as well. The threats to Mediterranean security are clearly felt most acutely in southern Europe. However, it would be wrong, a German official suggested, to see these threats solely as southern European concerns. Germany wants to extend stability both to the East *and* to the South. This requires a parallel process in the EU and NATO. These two processes should be complementary and need to be closely coordinated in order to avoid duplication of effort.

One of the key difficulties that emerged during the conference was the problem of identifying the threats in and to the Mediterranean region. Many argued that the end of the Cold War has changed the security situation dramatically. Europe is not, either today or tomorrow, facing a single overriding security threat. Rather, one participant argued, there is a very peculiar threat from countries that find themselves in a transition stage: a transition from authoritarian to democratic systems, from command to market economies, from inward-looking to outward-looking economies. However, in security terms, the Mediterranean is fragmented.

Many of the security problems in the southern Mediterranean have their roots in the lack of economic development and the economic disparities within the region. Moreover, economic development and population growth are directly linked to the migration facing Europe. Economic underdevelopment in the Maghreb and North Africa, together with a population growth of 2–3 percent per year, is creating strong pressures for migration to Europe. This migration, however, is not just a French or Spanish problem; it affects all of Europe. The dimensions of the migration problem have increased significantly in recent years. As a result, several participants suggested, Europe needs to rethink its aid and immigration policies. However, Europe is just now beginning to recognize the dimensions and urgency of the problem.

The question of Islamic fundamentalism was also a major focal point of discussion. There was general agreement among the participants that Islamic fundamentalism is a concern in the Mediterranean region. But many participants were also quick to point out that a more careful evaluation and a more nuanced approach to Islamic groups is required. The tendency of Western countries to label all Islamic groups as extremists and terrorists is inaccurate and counterproductive and contributes to the perception that NATO is seeking a new enemy.   Several non-NATO-country representatives cited the remarks by former NATO Secretary General Willy Claes about the threat from Muslim fundamentalism as an illustration of this tendency—though NATO participants were quick to point out that Claes had recanted his statement.

Islamic fundamentalism, several dialogue country participants argued, should be clearly demarcated from political Islam, which can be characterized by terrorism and extremism. Islamic extremism emerges in countries, they pointed out, where the regimes lack legitimacy. There was thus a close connection between the rise of political Islam and economic and political reform. If one wants to reduce the influence of radical Islam, then one has to remove the social and political conditions that nurture and foster its development. The West should encourage and support the emergence of nonradical moderate Islamic forces in the region.

The extent to which Islamic movements represent a threat for Europe was a subject of sharp disagreement among the participants. On the one hand, some participants stressed the danger of political Islam. However, one participant argued that the real problem resides with renegade regimes, which share a certain set of symptoms: authoritarian government; fascination with weapons of mass destruction; attraction to terrorism; contempt for western values and little regard for their own. These regimes include those of Iran, Iraq, Libya, and Syria. The success of these nations, some argued, could lead to other countries in the region falling into the same trap.

It was important, however, to distinguish between political Islam and radical Islam, several participants argued. The success of political Islam is closely connected to the lack of legitimacy of many of the regimes in the region. The problem is that in many countries in the Middle East and North Africa alternative political forces are repressed. This means that there is no alternative to the ruling regimes other than radical Islam. It is thus important for the West to encourage and support the emergence of nonradical, moderate Islamic forces in the region.

The second session focused on non-NATO perspectives on Mediterranean security. In order to frame the discussion, an Egyptian
participant offered three different perspectives of Mediterranean
security as seen from the south. The first perspective, which he
termed "idealist," does not differ significantly from the Western view
of the Mediterranean as a problem area. The second viewpoint can
be thought of as "cooperative" or "collaborative." Those who advo-
cate this approach may differ in their concept of the Mediterranean
region, but they do not disagree on the solutions to its problems. In
essence, they believe that if you can't beat the West, then join it.

The third viewpoint is the "rejectionist" or "radical" view. Advocates
of this position believe that the threats come from the North and the
West. The problem is not with the Mediterranean itself. From the
"radical" perspective, there are three major threats: first, a physical
threat; second, the threat from intra-Western rivalries which could
fuel conflicts in the Mediterranean; third, the cultural threat from
Western values.

Israel is still seen by some Arab countries as the main threat to security in the region. But as one Egyptian participant noted, the threats
in the region are changing. Since the early 1980s, the Arab-Israeli
conflict has not been the real source of conflict in the Middle East.
The most recent security threats—the Gulf War, the Iran-Iraq war,
the civil war in Yemen and Sudan—had nothing to do with the Arab-
Israeli conflict. The key security problems in the Middle East today,
he suggested, are ethnic conflicts, as evidenced in Iran, Iraq, and Sudan. Economic disparities are also a source of threat.

There was a general consensus among the participants that the threats to the region are, in fact, quite diverse. They include

- economic disparities and inequality
- population growth/migration
- depletion of resources, especially water
- Islamic extremism
- the proliferation of weapons of mass destruction.

These problems are interrelated and have to be dealt with at the regional level.

A number of participants suggested that the main threats to the region are internal, not external. They arise out of the lack of economic development on the one hand, and the lack of legitimacy of many of the governments in the region on the other. Not all participants, however, agreed with this proposition. The West, a North African participant argued, tends to see the conflicts in North Africa as internal problems, but the West also bears some responsibility for these conflicts. For example, the conflict between Morocco and Algeria over the Sahara can be attributed in part to a very old agenda that was played out by the colonial powers.

Several participants also pointed to what they termed a cultural threat. In the Middle East, one Egyptian participant noted, a high priority is placed on developing and maintaining indigenous national cultures. New states are being created on the basis of very old cultures. Many in the Middle East resent what they perceive as an effort by the West to impose or promote so called "correct" values. The West's ability to control and dominate international communications allows it to spread its influence and its values. Most participants, however, rejected the Huntingtonian thesis of a "clash of civilizations" as both inaccurate and conceptually flawed.

ECONOMIC DEVELOPMENT AND DEMOCRATIZATION

Most participants agreed that the main threats to security in the region are internal and have their roots in economic disparities and lack of economic development. The lack of economic development exacerbates social and political tensions in the region. The escalation of these tensions could result in increased immigration and have direct political consequences for Europe, especially southern Europe. Thus, Europe has a strong interest in ensuring that the transitions in the Maghreb and the Middle East proceed in a stable and smooth manner.

The desire to avoid a spillover from economic and social tensions in the region is at the heart of the European Union's strategy toward the Mediterranean. The EU's strategy is designed to accelerate economic, social, and political change in the region without destabilizing it. The main goals of the EU's strategy are

- development of a full-fledged manufacturing sector that would enable the countries of the region to increase their exports and earn foreign currency;

- promotion of greater interregional trade;

- creation of a Euro-Mediterranean free-trade area similar to that created by the North American Free Trade Agreement (NAFTA);

- development of strong civil societies; and

- improvement of educational standards.

Implementing this strategy will be a long and difficult process, an EU representative acknowledged. But, a European representative emphasized, Europe has no real choice. It has to pursue such a policy if the economic, social, and political tensions in the region are to be defused. Moreover, to succeed, this policy has to be long-term and sustained.

Few participants disagreed with these remarks in principle. The real question, as several participants noted, is how such a policy should be implemented in practice. As one American participant pointed out, there is a potential conflict—or tension—in Western policy. On the one hand, the West wants stability in the region. On the other, it favors economic reform and political liberalization. But these processes, he pointed out, are inherently destabilizing. In many cases, Islamic opposition movements would be the direct beneficiaries of political liberalization. This, to be sure, is not an argument against political reform, but it does highlight the dilemmas inherent in Western policy.

In addition, many of the most politically conservative regimes in the region are supported by the United States and the West. Promoting political liberalization in these countries would directly undermine these regimes. This might not be a problem in the case of autocratic regimes that are regarded as enemies (e.g., Iraq), but it does pose problems for friendly regimes such as Saudi Arabia or Morocco. Managing this dilemma could prove difficult.

Several participants, however, argued that economic reform and political liberalization did not necessarily have to be destabilizing— as the cases of Eastern Europe and Latin America underscore. In these areas, foreign investment and economic assistance have generally been welcomed. On balance, they argued, the record worldwide suggests that outside influences have not been all that destabilizing and economic and political integration have not been that detrimental.

The dichotomy between economic development and democracy is a false one, a European Union official suggested. In the end there is simply no alternative to economic change. If the countries of the Middle East and North Africa do not manage their economic problems, there will be serious social and political consequences. The unemployment problems are so great, he stressed, that without a growth rate of 8–10 percent per year, these problems could not be managed. The key question is not *whether* the countries of the Mediterranean should be integrated into the world economy but *how* they should be integrated. Integration is a necessity in order to attract foreign investment, which these countries need in order to stabilize and modernize their economies. Increased regional trade between the North and South is also necessary. The EU proposal to set up a Euro-Mediterranean free-trade area by the year 2010 would greatly facilitate regional trade and would also stimulate a fundamental shift in investment patterns.

One European participant pointed out that the time factor is important. Economic solutions could take decades. But the resolution of the region's political problems cannot wait. The basic political problem is that many of the regimes in the region *lack political legitimacy.* In many countries, moreover, the armed forces are instruments of internal repression. This poses difficult dilemmas for Western policy. The Algerian regime, for instance, supports NATO's Mediterranean initiative because it sees the initiative as support against its internal enemies. Other regimes, on the other hand, see the NATO initiative as an attempt to interfere in their internal affairs.

Several North African participants cautioned that cooperation with the dialogue countries should not be made conditional on democracy. Democracy in the Middle East, they argued, will never be the same as democracy in Europe or in the United States. Yet these regimes will still be democratic. The form of democracy, however, will be different and a product of the special indigenous conditions in the Middle East and North Africa. There is a tendency in the West to see many of the regimes in the Mediterranean as authoritarian. But public opinion is important in these countries and has a powerful impact in some cases, even if this is not readily visible to outsiders.

CRISIS PREVENTION: THE ROLE OF WESTERN INSTITUTIONS

The conference devoted considerable attention to the role that various institutions—including NATO—could play in preventing and containing regional crises in the Mediterranean. There was a general consensus that most of the threats to regional stability are economic and political, not military. Thus, the main instruments in preventing crises in the region should be economic and political. This strongly suggests that the EU should play the lead role in trying to contain and prevent crises in the region.

However, the EU, one European participant pointed out, does not have a common policy toward the region. It has a *common economic policy* but not a broad common policy. For instance, it has no common policy toward political Islam. There is also no common policy toward Algeria. For this reason, it is difficult to define a common policy toward U.S. involvement in the region. First, Europe has to define a common European policy. Then it could define its policy toward the United States. But at the moment, such a common European policy does not exist.

Even in the case of the Euro-Mediterranean partnership, he suggested, the objectives are not clear. The main objective of the partnership is to create a Euro-Mediterranean free-trade area. It is not intended to be a new CSCM. But this distinction has to be made clear. Otherwise, there is no reason not to invite the United States, which is a key regional actor in the Mediterranean. However, if the objective of the partnership is to create a Mediterranean NAFTA, then exclusion of the United States makes sense.

Several participants raised the issue of the role of the OSCE and the possible revival of CSCM. Yet it is not clear that OSCE mechanisms can be easily transferred to the Mediterranean. As one Italian participant pointed out, the contexts are quite different. The type of intervention that the OSCE conducted in Estonia regarding the Russian minority would be difficult to do in the Mediterranean context. Would any Arab country be willing to accept such interference? The EU and OSCE efforts to dampen Hungarian-Romanian tensions provide another example. Would any Arab country accept similar interference?

Some participants, moreover, questioned whether the OSCE is really relevant given its ineffectiveness in Bosnia and inability to prevent the outbreak of conflict there. But, as one American participant noted, the OSCE was not originally intended as an instrument for crisis prevention. Rather, its main purpose has been—and continues to be—to establish a set of standards and norms that would apply to all states. These standards have been largely ignored by the communist states in Europe for many years. But ultimately they prevailed. It might be useful, therefore, to think of a CSCM more in terms of a general framework for establishing general norms and standards of behavior rather than as a mechanism for crisis management.

In addition, there is the question of the U.S. role in the region. Several participants questioned whether it was prudent to exclude the United States from the Euro-Med conference in Barcelona. After all, the United States is an important actor in the region. French opposition has been an important factor but, several participants pointed out, it is only part of the reason for the exclusion of the United States. The larger reason is the ambiguity about the focus and purpose of the Barcelona conference.

Some participants, however, questioned whether the United States is truly interested in the Mediterranean. The United States clearly has interests in the Balkans and eastern Mediterranean but, they asked, is it really interested in the western Mediterranean? At the moment, it seems more preoccupied with the Balkans. But as several American participants pointed out, the United States has been a Mediterranean power for 200 years and it is likely to remain one for the foreseeable future. At the moment, its main focus is on the Balkans,

Middle East, and eastern Mediterranean, but the boundaries between these areas are breaking down in the post–Cold War period. It is no longer possible to rigidly compartmentalize security problems in the Mediterranean. Moreover, the growing EU involvement in the Mediterranean will inevitably draw NATO—and the United States—more deeply into the Mediterranean, including the western Mediterranean.

The critical issue, several participants argued, is what the division of labor should be between the various institutions in the region. Who should do what? Some thought NATO should play a lead role in the region. A French participant argued, however, that this option is unrealistic. Moreover, it is not in harmony with the U.S. policy of selective disengagement. Neither the United States nor NATO is prepared, he suggested, to commit substantial resources to the area. Moreover, it is important to avoid turning the Mediterranean into a North-South issue.

The alternative is for Europe alone to take the lead. But Europe does not have a unified view toward the Mediterranean. It is hard, the French participant argued, to get the Germans or Danes interested in the region. Moreover, Bosnia showed that the Europeans still need the United States. Thus, the solution, he suggested, is to strengthen *both* the European and the NATO pillars. A division of labor is necessary. NATO should deal with the Greek-Turkish dispute, while the European Union should deal with the social and economic dimensions of security. But the Mediterranean, he warned, should not become a "NATO area." At the same time, it is important to increase U.S. consciousness about the importance of the Mediterranean.

NATO'S ROLE IN THE MEDITERRANEAN

The preceding discussion led naturally into a discussion of NATO's role and NATO's Mediterranean initiative. To help frame the discussion a NATO official outlined the purposes of NATO's Mediterranean initiative. NATO's role in the Mediterranean, he explained, is experimental and incremental. NATO is still "testing the waters," as he put it. During the Cold War, NATO had paid attention to the Mediterranean. But this had been within the context of the Soviet naval threat.

The end of the Cold War has forced NATO to change its approach. With the deepening EU involvement in the Mediterranean, NATO also has to begin to pay greater attention to the region. After the Italian proposal to discuss Mediterranean security at the Brussels NATO summit of January 1994, the impetus for NATO's Mediterranean initiative came from Spain, but the initiative now has the support of all of NATO. The Mediterranean initiative has three major objectives:

- to contribute to security and stability in the Mediterranean;

- to promote mutual understanding among NATO and the countries of the Mediterranean; and

- to counteract misperceptions about the Alliance.

The initial round of the dialogue began in February 1995 and was designed to address suspicions and public perceptions. It was focused largely on information activities. There are several areas of possible future cooperation. These include

- continuing information activities;
- scientific and environmental affairs;
- military exchanges and exercises.

Participants in the conference were divided about the utility and effectiveness of NATO's initiative. Several non-NATO participants— and some participants from NATO states—expressed skepticism about NATO's ability to contribute much in the Mediterranean. The main problems in the region, they pointed out, are economic and political, not military. The EU is thus better suited to dealing with these problems than NATO is. In addition, mistrust of NATO is strong among segments of the elites in the dialogue countries. Many elites in the region view NATO's new interest in the Mediterranean with suspicion, if not alarm. They see it as a reflection of NATO's search for a "new enemy" now that the Cold War is over. There is thus a serious risk that the initiative might serve to divide the Arab world.

It was unlikely, an American official suggested, that NATO would become deeply involved in the Mediterranean unless a significant military threat emerged. The social, economic, and political implications of the problems of the Mediterranean are of secondary concern to NATO. Moreover, several NATO allies prefer to see Mediterranean issues dealt with bilaterally rather than in NATO. The exception is the Greek-Turkish dispute, which is of great concern to NATO and to the United States.

Other participants, however, took a more positive view of NATO's role. They agreed that NATO has to be sensitive to Arab suspicions and concerns. They also agreed that the EU should play the primary role in the region. However, this does not mean, they argued, that NATO could ignore the Mediterranean. NATO's outreach to the East has to be accompanied by an outreach to the South. The question is not *whether* NATO should be involved in the Mediterranean, but *how* it should be involved. What should the content of NATO's initiative be? Should the initiative concentrate largely on promoting a security dialogue with the nations of the Middle East and Maghreb? Or should it also involve defense cooperation? Is the idea of PfP for the Mediterranean, as suggested by some Alliance officials, premature? Or is it an idea whose time has come?

These questions produced no clear consensus. Many participants, especially those from the non-NATO dialogue countries, cautioned against moving too quickly. NATO, they stressed, is still viewed with considerable suspicion in many circles in the Middle East and Maghreb. Thus, NATO should first concentrate on changing its image in the Arab world. This will take time and cannot be done overnight. The first phase of NATO's initiative should be exploratory, a representative from Mauritania suggested, and should concentrate on threat perceptions. The main purpose should be to "de-demonize" NATO.

Several participants from non-NATO dialogue states suggested that the initiative should be broadened to include countries such as Algeria, Syria, and Libya. Many Western participants, however, felt that inviting these countries at this stage would be premature. NATO has to be careful, they asserted, that it does not end up bolstering weak, illegitimate regimes or being perceived as strengthening autocracy in the region. The Algerian government, for instance, several participants pointed out, wants to be invited in order to bolster its sense of legitimacy in its struggle with radical Islamic forces within the country. Thus, NATO has to be careful to whom it extends the initiative, lest it end up becoming a pawn in a domestic struggle for power.

The discussion suggested that NATO needs a better understanding of the views and perceptions of the non-NATO dialogue countries. What do they really want? How do they see their relationship with NATO? What are their long-term goals? More systematic research and analysis are needed on these issues, several participants stressed.

The discussion also suggested the need for close coordination and harmonization of NATO policy and EU policy in the Mediterranean. The two policies should be complementary and be designed to promote greater regional stability. While the EU should play the leading role, the growing EU involvement in the Mediterranean will inevitably draw NATO more deeply into the region. Hence, NATO will have to develop a comprehensive policy toward the region and clarify the objectives of its Mediterranean initiative.

At the same time, NATO will need to revamp its own command structure and decisionmaking process to allow it to more effectively deal with the new challenges it will face in the coming decade, many of which could be in the South. The presentation by Admiral Leighton Smith, Commander-in-Chief of AFSOUTH, highlighted the degree to which NATO's responsibilities and interests in the Southern region have become broader and more complex since the end of the Cold War. AFSOUTH's areas of strategic interest today extend well beyond NATO territory. They include the territory of the former Soviet Union, North Africa, and the Middle East. Bosnia is only one of a number of potential crises in AFSOUTH's area of responsibility, Smith stressed.   The Caucasus remains highly unstable. The instability in North Africa is a potential problem not only for Europe but also for NATO and the United States.

The expansion of AFSOUTH's areas of strategic interests and responsibilities raises important questions about AFSOUTH's role and the need to adapt NATO's command structure to the post–Cold War era. This command structure, as one American participant noted, is largely a function of the Cold War and is heavily oriented toward the Central Front. However, the main security threats today are not on the Central Front but on Europe's periphery and beyond Europe's borders. NATO, therefore, needs to be transformed and restructured to better deal with these new threats. This process should include a streamlining of the command structure. This task, the conference discussions suggested, should become a top NATO priority.

LIST OF PARTICIPANTS

I. UNITED STATES

John Berry, Director, European Policy, Office of the Secretary of Defense

Graham Fuller, RAND

David Gompert, RAND

Jerrold Green, RAND

Shireen Hunter, Senior Research Fellow, Centre for European Policy Studies

F. Stephen Larrabee, RAND

Ian Lesser, RAND

Steve R. Nugent, Embassy of the United States of America, Brussels

Alison Shanck, Director of Education, Atlantic Council of the U.S.

Carla Thorson (RAND Rapporteur)

Gregory Treverton, RAND

John Van Oudenaren, RAND

II. NORTH ATLANTIC TREATY ORGANIZATION

H.E. Ambassador Sergio Balanzino, Deputy Secretary General

H.E. Ambassador Carlos Miranda, Permanent Representative of Spain on the North Atlantic Council

H.E. Ambassador Dr. Hermann Freiherr von Richtofen, Permanent Representative of Germany on the North Atlantic Council

H.E. Ambassador Robert E. Hunter, Permanent Representative of the United States on the North Atlantic Council

Min. Plen. Stefano Starace Janfolla, Permanent Representative of Italy on the North Atlantic Council

H.E. Ambassador Vassilis Zafiropoulos, Permanent Representative of Greece on the North Atlantic Council

H.E. Ambassador Jose Martins Da Cruz, Permanent Representative of Portugal on the North Atlantic Council

H.E. Ambassador Gunnar Riberholdt, Permanent Representative of Denmark on the North Atlantic Council

Admiral Leighton Smith, Jr., Commander in Chief, Allied Forces Southern Europe

Vice Admiral Nuno G. Vieira Matias, CINC, Iberian Atlantic Area

Brig. Gen. A. Arena, Deputy Assistant Director, Arms Control and Military Cooperation, Plans and Policy Division, IMS

Vice Admiral M. R. Gretton, SACLANTREPEUR

Rear Admiral Ralph L. Tindal, Deputy CINC, Iberian Atlantic Area

Commander Jim Carr, CINCSOUTH Office, HQ AFSOUTH

Lt. Col. Pierfranco Maida, Air Aide to CINCSOUTH, Executive Assistant, HQ AFSOUTH

Captain Marc Van Dijk, Chief of Public Information Division, HQ AFSOUTH

Slt. Carlos M.T.P.C. Peres, ADC to CINCIBERLANT

Dr. Jamie Shea, NATO Spokesman and Deputy Director, Information and Press

François le Blevennec, NATO Office of Information and Press

Margaret C. Pearson, Head, Planning and Production Section, NATO Office of Information and Press

Nicola de Santis, Officer for Southern and Eastern Mediterranean Countries, NATO Office of Information and Press

Spyros Philippas, Liaison Officer for Greece, NATO Office of Information and Press

Werner Bauwens, Liaison Officer for Belgium, NATO Office of Information and Press

Jose Maria Lopez Navarro, Liaison Officer for Spain, NATO Office of Information and Press

Mrs. Emel Uresin, Liaison Officer for Turkey, NATO Office of Information and Press

Peter Jenner, Director, NATO Review, NATO Office of Information and Press

Allen Keiswetter, Deputy Assistant Secretary General for Political Affairs, Director, Political Directorate

Marcel Leroy, Head, NATO Multilateral and Regional Affairs Section

Greta Gunnarsdottir, Political Officer, NATO Political Affairs Division

Catherine McArdle Kelleher, Personal Representative of the U.S. Secretary of Defense in Europe, Defense Advisor to the U.S. Mission to NATO

Leo Verbruggen, Executive Secretary, Executive Secretariat

Robert Pearson, Deputy Permanent Representative of the U.S. on the North Atlantic Council

Creena Lavery, United Kingdom Delegation to NATO

Jette Nordam, Counsellor, Permanent Representation of Denmark to NATO

Bernhard Schlagheck, First Secretary, Permanent Representation of Germany to NATO

Mario Boffo, Counsellor, Permanent Representation of Italy on the North Atlantic Council

Evangelos Damianakis, Counsellor, Permanent Representation of Greece on the North Atlantic Council

Yunus Demirer, Third Secretary, Permanent Representation of Turkey on the North Atlantic Council

Johan Vibe, Norwegian Permanent Delegation to NATO

III. EUROPEAN UNION

Pierre Étienne Champenois, Director General of Common Foreign and Security Policy Unit, General Secretariat of the EU Council

Luigi Mattiolo, CFSP Unit, Council of the European Union

Eberhard Rhein, Director of Mediterranean, Near East and Middle East Affairs, EU Commission

IV. NORTH ATLANTIC ASSEMBLY

John Borawski, Director, Political Committee

Catherine Guicherd, Director, Civilian Affairs Committee

V. WEU

Guido Lenzi, Director, WEU Institute for Security Studies, Paris

VI. NATO MEMBER COUNTRIES

BELGIUM

Anne Herman, SEVI Institute, Brussels

Pascal Leys, Deputy Head, Western European Countries Directorate, Ministry of Foreign Affairs

Luc Terlimck, Head, Western European Countries Directorate, Ministry of Foreign Affairs

FRANCE

Pierre Lellouche, Member of the National Assembly, Paris

I. Valentini, Délégation aux Affaires Stratégiques, Ministry of Defense

GERMANY

Heinz-Jürgen Axt, Gerhard-Mercator-Universität, Duisburg

Werner Ruf, University of Kassel, Kassel

GREAT BRITAIN

Zahid Nawaz, Office of Bruce George, MP, Vice Chairman, Defence Committee, House of Commons

John Roper, Royal Institute of International Affairs, London

GREECE

Thanos Veremis, Director, Hellenic Foundation for Defense and Foreign Policy, Athens

ITALY

Roberto Aliboni, Director of Studies, Istituto Affari Internazionali (IAI), Rome

Gianni Bonvicini, Director, IAI, Rome

Maurizio Cremasco, Senior Researcher, IAI, Rome

Marta Dassu, Director, Centro Studi di Politica Internazionale, Rome

Riccardo Guariglia, Consul General, Consulate of Italy, Brussels

Major General Renzo Romano, Director, Joint Services Staff College, Rome

PORTUGAL

Alvaro de Vasconcelos, Director, Instituto de Estudos Estratégicos e Internacionais (IEEI), Lisbon

SPAIN

Javier Rupérez, Speaker for Foreign Affairs in the House, Popular Party, Madrid

TURKEY

Ali Karaosmanoglu, Bilkent University, Ankara

VII. NON-NATO MEDITERRANEAN COUNTRIES

EGYPT

Abdel Monem Said Aly, Director, Al Ahram Center for Political and Strategic Studies (ACPSS), Cairo

H.E. Ambassador Mouhammad Chabane, Ambassador of Egypt to Belgium

Mourad Ibrahim El Dessouki, Head of Military Unit, ACPSS, Cairo

Mohamed El Zorkany, Chargé d'Affaires, Embassy of Egypt

ISRAEL

H.E. Ambassador Mordechai Drory, Ambassador of Israel to Belgium

Dr. Ephraim Kam, Deputy Head, Jaffe Center for Strategic Studies (JCSS), Tel Aviv

Professor Zeev Ma'oz, Head, Jaffe Center for Strategic Studies (JCSS), Tel Aviv

Professor Shmuel Sandler, Senior Researcher, BESA (Begin Sadat) Center for Strategic Studies, Bar-Ilan University, Ramat Gan

MAURITANIA

Cheikh Saad Bou Kamara, University of Novakchott

H.E. Ambassador Ahmed Uld Sid'Ahmed, Ambassador of Mauritania to Belgium

MOROCCO

M'Hammed Dasser, Vice Dean, Université Mohammed V., Faculté des Sciences Juridiques, Économiques et Sociales, Rabat-Agdal

Adelghani Kadmiri, Dean, Université Mohammed V., Faculté des Sciences Juridiques, Économiques et Sociales, Rabat-Agdal

H.E. Ambassador Mohamed Guedira, Ambassador of Morocco to Belgium

TUNISIA

Professor Khalifa Chater, Vice President, AIE, Tunis

Ambassador Rachid Driss, President, Association des Études Internationales (AIE), Tunis

OCTOBER 15   Arrival of Participants

8:00 pm   *Dinner*

OCTOBER 16

8:45–9:00 am   **OPENING SESSION**

Opening Remarks by Conference Chairmen

F. Stephen Larrabee and
Greg Treverton

9:00–10:30 am   Keynote Address by H.E. Ambassador Sergio
Balanzino, Deputy Secretary General of
NATO

**Mediterranean Security and Transatlantic
Relations**

Presentation: Pierre Lellouche (France)

10:30-11:00 am   *Coffee Break*

11:00 am–12:30 pm   **New Dimensions of Mediterranean Security:
Western Perspectives**

Presentation: Ian Lesser (RAND)

Response: Javier Rupérez (Spain)

12:30–2:00 pm   *Lunch*

Address by Admiral Leighton Smith, Jr.,
Commander-in-Chief, Allied Forces Southern
Europe

2:00–3:30 pm   **SESSION II**

New Dimensions of Mediterranean Security: Non-NATO Perspectives

Chairman: Guido Lenzi (WEU)

Presentation: Abdel Monem Said Aly (Egypt)

Response: Rachid Driss (Tunisia)

Response: Zeev Ma'oz (Israel)

3:30–4:00 pm   *Coffee Break*

4:00–5:30 pm   **Economic, Political, and Social Change: Implications for Security**

Presentation: Eberhard Rhein (EU Commission)

Response: Jerrold Green (RAND)

Response: Werner Ruf (Germany)

8:00 pm   *Dinner*

Address by Ambassador Robert E. Hunter, Permanent Representative of the United States on the North Atlantic Council

OCTOBER 17

9:00–10:30 am   **SESSION III**

Crisis Prevention in the Mediterranean: Institutional Responses and Political Instruments

Chairman: David Gompert

Presentation: Alvaro de Vasconcelos (Portugal)

Response: Roberto Aliboni (Italy)

Response: John Roper (UK)

10:30–11:00 am   *Coffee Break*

11:00 am–12:30 pm   **NATO's Mediterranean Initiative: Content and Future Prospects**

Presentation: Marcel Leroy (NATO)

Response: Ambassador Driss (Tunisia)
Response: Mourad Ibrahim El Dessouki
(Egypt)

12:30–2:00 pm   *Lunch*

2:00–3:30 pm   **SESSION IV**

**Regional Influences on the Mediterranean:
The Balkans, Eastern Mediterranean, and
Middle East**

Chairman: John Roper (UK)

Presentation: Graham Fuller (RAND)

Response: Thanos Veremis (Greece)
Response: Ali Karaosmanoglu (Turkey)

3:30–4:00 pm   *Coffee Break*

4:00–5:30 pm   **Wrap-Up: Future Policy Directions**

David Gompert (RAND)

Guido Lenzi (WEU)

Khalifa Chater (Tunisia)